Conversations
with Prisoners

A window into the lives of our brothers and sisters

Jack Kennevan

VITALITY

buzz, bliss + books

in gratitude to our VATRONS
who breathed life into this book
by pre-ordering their copy

Sue Antoinette & Russ Martin, Helen Buswinka
Sharon Byrnes, William Coleman, Beth & Dan Corbo
Mary & Tim Cronin, Jessi Deaso, Mary Duennes
Kathy Eby, Denise & Mike Eck, Sherri Elmore
Ruth Foote, Mary Beth Fritsch, Peg Halpin
Mike & Fran Harmon, Matthew Klooster
Spencer Kociba, Patricia R Leigh
Allie & George Maggini, Kim & Mark McLaughlin
Alice Michels, Marianne Mundy
Krista Powers & Patrick Flerlage, Peg Niehaus
Judy & Fred Reuter, Mary Ann Roncker
Judy & Bill Sandquist, Mary & Bob Schneider
Lucy Schultz, Jodi & Wayne Shircliff, Brian Shircliff
Velda Smiley, Tonia Smith, Peggy & Dan St. Clair
Beverly Thomas, Thomas VonderBrink
Amy & Steve Whitlatch, John Williams
Damon Wilson, Carol Yeazell
Carol T & Bruce Yeazell

Jack has generously offered this collection of letters to be published with proceeds supporting VITALITY Cincinnati's holistic mission and ministry, just as his pastor Richard Bollman, S.J. has done with his *Selected Homilies*. In honor of Jack, VITALITY will make a donation of a portion of the proceeds of *Conversations with Prisoners* to Transforming Jail Ministries.

CONTENTS

A few words of introduction from Jack

Dear Brothers and Sisters,

In 2003 I retired from Covington Catholic High School. Although I spent the next year as interim principal at Purcell-Marian, my years of work in education came to an end and I began to consider how I could continue to serve, to discern where God was leading me.

During my years at Covington Catholic, I became acquainted with an individual serving a sentence in Kentucky. I would visit from time to time, but mostly I wrote to him. He kept insisting that I should do that as a ministry so that was in the back of my mind.

I decided to explore how I could do be a part of prison ministry. I met with Jack Marsh, a prison chaplain at the jail. Since I was a Catholic, he put me in touch with Fr. Mark Schmieder. After our first jail visit, Fr. Mark said, "Jack, you can do this." And that is how I became a prison chaplain.

In 2007 some of us met with Jack Marsh and Transforming Jail Ministry was born, and I became a part of that movement. I began to make a weekly visit to the Hamilton County Justice Center and meet with those that had asked for a chaplain. At first I met with men and women, though as our ministry expanded, I met with men only. For these visits I took along a Catholic paper, but soon sensed it was not that helpful so the teacher in me said, "Why not prepare 'lessons'?" so I began to write a letter including reflections from books I was reading or ideas I heard from others, reflections that I thought would be helpful in response to what I was hearing from them.

So on April 21, 2007, I wrote my first letter. As I shared these with the prisoners, I would write on the copies reflections from our sharings so they would have that to mull over in the coming weeks in between our visits. Gradually, more prisoners asked to see me and asked for copies of my letters, both men and women. When some of them were moved to prisons, they wrote to me and asked that I send them a copy of my biweekly letters. These here in this book are a few of the 290 letters I wrote over the years until COVID-19 (and age) ended my weekly visits.

I hope you'll grow with me.

Your brother,
Jack

A few words from Helen Buswinka, friend and curator of Jack's letters

"I'm just a scribe," Jack offers as we sit at his dining room table on a sunny October afternoon. "I take what I've heard and I share it," he continues. Jack's description of his work belies the rich layers of life from which these letters spring. Teacher, counselor, principal and coach; these were Jack's professional pursuits, and the knowledge and values of those ventures certainly informed the relationships he built with the men at the Justice Center. But so, too, do his younger years as a student. He recalls his mentors fondly, learning from them not only what they had to teach, but also how to build a caring relationship. And so, too, does the heartfelt way he approaches life. Whether it is a book, a homily, a personal experience, or a story he has heard, Jack explores the matter until it has become part of him. "You have to have a way of making it yours," he remarks. So yes, maybe "just a scribe," but truly a scribe of life.

It has been more than fifty years since I first met Jack Kennevan. My late husband Pete, along with Jack's wife Jean, and several other couples, were part of a six week Lenten discussion group that evolved into decades of dinners, word games, scintillating conversation, crazy antics, and above all, friendship. We took off for weekend getaways just to have time enough to talk about the deep things of life and play with words. True friends and generous, one weekend Jack and Jean babysat our three small children so Pete and I could have time away.

Conversations those young years, of course, included talking about our children, our jobs, and life's exigencies. But the notion of service was never far from the conversation, and often its center. No wonder, years later as we left our careers and moved into retirement, Jack and Pete both felt the call to befriend those who were imprisoned. They came to this in different ways, Pete saying, "I've done other work but I haven't yet visited the imprisoned," and Jack saying, "I've been a teacher, counselor and coach, but this is a road not yet taken." Work yet to be done; roads yet to be taken.

Pete joined the Kairos Prison Ministry becoming part of a team of men building relationships with the residents of high security prisons. Later, as a Stephen Minister he would visit individuals monthly for as long as their sentences lasted. The young residents came to see him as a caring grandfather. Jack took a different path, serving as chaplain to those jailed but not yet sentenced. "We had something in common," said Jack. "We all stumble. We were just brothers."

Always a wordsmith, it is no surprise that Jack began to write letters to the men he visited, using each letter as an impetus to conversation and serving as a point for reflection afterward. Sometimes Jack drew a sketch on the letter in order to more fully illustrate an idea. So natural is this way of being to Jack that he began to sketch for me as I asked him to describe the setting in which he visited these men. I can imagine these letters, folded up in a pocket or tucked into a book, offering counsel long after the visit as the men awaited sentencing.

I am edified by reading these letters. Though not confined, I also have decisions to make, purposes to keep, and life to ponder. So do you. The topics are timeless and universal. And there is more. In *Conversations with Prisoners* Jack Kennevan offers the reader a way to see as he does; to encounter all he meets as brothers and sisters. "Keep an open mind, walk in their shoes, be nonjudgemental," Jack counsels. This book is an invitation to do so.

Jack's letters with prisoners

April 21, 2007

Dear Brothers and Sisters,

During my weekly visits, I usually bring you a copy of the Cincinnati Diocesan newspaper, the *Catholic Telegraph*. The other day the teacher in me (I first began teaching in December, 1954) kicked in! An inner voice said, why don't you share some of the words that really are thought provoking? The following is an attempt to share some insights I received from books I have read while being a substitute teacher and/or from personal reading.

My hope is that you will read each of these quotes (once for the head and a second time for the heart) and reflect on the content of each. You may even want to share some of these thoughts with those members of your family and friends to whom you write.

"Wise men talk because they have something to say; fools because they to have to say something."

Plato

"The greatest discovery of any generation is that a human being can alter his life by altering his attitude."

William James

"In today already walks tomorrow."

Samuel Coleridge

Note: The space below this page is for your reflections!

Your brother in Our Lord,

Volunteer Prison Chaplain

April 27, 2007

Dear Brothers and Sisters,

Now is a good time to ask, how am I using my time? How am I preparing myself, that is, what plan or plans am I making as I await sentencing and what will I do with my time after a judgment is made?

It is my hope and prayer that you will factor in a lot of time in prayer, reflection, writing, and dialoguing with the significant others in your life.

Always stayed tuned to God!

God does answer "knee-mail!"

When you pray you might want to dedicate each day to God on behalf of those special people in your life. I would like to suggest that as you put on your shirt (top) in the morning, you may want to kiss it and say to yourself, inspired by Colossions 3:

> "Lord, today I clothe myself in your spirit of
> care and compassion for others. Help me to be
> a true and faithful follower of your way of life."

The month of May is just around the comer. Therefore, Mother's Day is not far off. Now is the time to prepare and to send mom a love letter.

Your brother in Our Lord,

Volunteer Prison Chaplain

May 4, 2007

Dear Brothers and Sisters,

Sometimes words aren't enough to convey our strong feelings. Whether we're trying to show sincere remorse, boundless gratitude, or great love, words alone may not capture our true meaning, and we are left wondering how to say what's in our hearts? However, these emotions need to be expressed. So it's important that we figure out a way.

SIMPLE STEPS:

> Let your actions speak for themselves. One small gesture can show what's in your Heart.

> Just say it. If you can't find the perfect words, just say how you feel. No one can argue with the honesty of your emotions!

Remember what William James said...how we can change our lives by altering our attitude!

Here is one final thought to ponder:

"Treat people as if they were what they ought to be, and you help them to become what they are capable of being!"

Goethe

Brothers and sisters, let us resolve to make this world a better place! We can be makers of peace!

Your brother in the Lord,

Prison Chaplain

June 1, 2007

Dear Brothers and Sisters,

Last week, I shared with you how I struggle with my relationship with God and, believe me, it is a struggle. I truly believe in God but so often He seems so far away. While at mass Sunday, I realized it is not so much me expecting God to do all work in my relationship, but I, you, we must do our part!

I cannot put into words the sense of community, a sense of a world seeking peace that I experienced. My brothers and sisters, we have work to do but if we commit, we can make this world, our families, and our communities places of peace and unity.

In closing I ask that you join me in praying for a speedy end to the war in Iraq. There are far too many innocent lives being lost on both sides. Pray also for a resolution of senseless dying of so many innocent people dying of hunger in Darfur.

And, finally let us pray for the courage and the conviction to be committed to being peacemakers.

Thank you and God bless you!

Your Brother in the Lord,

The Prison Chaplain

July 20, 2007

My brothers and sisters,

Please pray for me as I do for you. I pray especially for the gifts of wisdom, wise counsel, and above all compassionate listening. I truly believe by praying for one another and all those significant others and the "not-so-significant" others, we can help to make this a better world. Let us be creative and redeeming brothers and sisters with the Lord.

Your Prison Chaplain

July 27, 2007

Dear friends,

We all have these moments of doubts or our faith seems to wane. We just plain don't feel good about ourselves and our world seems to be coming apart. This mental and spiritual struggle challenges us to exercise our "faith muscles" and to deal with the reality of our situation. Change has and will occur. Just looking at the many changes that has and are taking place in our lives should encourage us that no obstacle is too big to overcome. I urge you to take time to read, reflect, write, dialogue and pray a lot. God answers all "knee-mail."

Your prison chaplain

Dear Brothers and Sisters,

When the door of your happiness was closed (detainment or incarceration) what has happened to or for you since that day? When the door of happiness closed, another opened but have you continued to look at the 'closed door' and have failed to look at the one that opened, your future. A beautiful future depends on forgetting the past. You can learn from the past; you cannot change the past. You will not be able to go forward in life as long as you have not overcome the errors of the past and all that hurt you. Forgive and set yourself free; let go, let God!

Last week I shared with you the directive that Our Lord gave us: "Ask and it will be given to you; seek and you will find; knock and the door will be opened to you." (Gospel of Matthew 7:7) For what are you searching? When the door opens what do expect to find? What will you or are you asking for at this time in your life? Is this request real or reasonable?

Dear brothers and sisters, more than anything I pray that you will seek peace and in the process discover who you are, how gifted you are and how you can make a difference in your life and in the lives of so many others.

May the peace, the presence and the power of God's love be yours to celebrate wildly!

Your chaplain

October 5, 2007

Dear Brothers and Sisters,

In last week's letter, I shared with my head, that is, I shared with you what I had been reading. There were many ideas contained in that letter that you may have missed. I wrote about the need to take care of your own behavior (needs) and not be so busy about advising others how they ought to live their lives ("Physician, cure yourself!").

Then there was the issue of "worry." Worry is like a rocking chair, it gives you something to do, but it doesn't get you anywhere! Instead of using your time worrying about issues you have no control of or worrying about situations you cannot change, use your time to deal with what you can actually could and should do.

My dear friends, that was last week's letter and as I said "I shared with my head." And that has concerned me very much. I keep thinking that perhaps I am not listening enough with my heart. Yes, I need to listen with my eyes and ears as well, but my concern is that I do too much of the talking. Perhaps, I thought, I need to take some quality time to listen to you. Therefore, when I am visiting with you perhaps you will share with me some ideas and experiences that you have experienced since your stay at the Justice Center. My hope is that you will have ideas that not only do you want to share them with me, but also you'd would like for me to share with others through my weekly letter.

I pray, my brothers and sisters, that God will always be

at the center of your lives and that you too will bring Him to be shared through your words and good deeds.

Namaste! I greet the God within you!

Chaplain

Dear Brothers and Sisters,

Staying with our topic, 're-journeying,' I have been thinking about how the telling of my life story and sharing it with others really does help both me and those who hear the story. While traveling to visit with my son and his family, I brought along Alan Alda's autobiography, *Never Have Your Dog Stuffed*. As I was reading his life story, I realized we all have stories to tell; it's a part of living! So many experiences to be shared and so many lessons to be learned from the storyteller.

When I think of telling one's story, so many questions come to mind. Where do I begin? Why begin there? For whom am I telling my story? What is the purpose of my sharing? From my earliest memories to the present, what are the most significant changes that have taken place and how have they changed me to who I am today?

As a grandparent, I never cease to be amazed how the grandchildren enjoy having stories read to them.

Storytelling is fascinating! Sometimes the grandkids seem to enjoy more the stories I make up about grandma and me. And, I must admit the purpose of these stories is purely to entertain. However, as I read Alan Alda's book, I was not so much entertained as I was informed. Alan had a very difficult childhood and struggled as a person, writer, actor and film director. He survived challenges and obstacles before becoming the successful person he is known to be today.

If I were to ask members of your family, your friends, and others whom you believe know you best, what would they say about you that is really telling? How do you think you would be described? As you ponder what might be said about you, I wonder if you feel like I do, a bit overwhelmed?

Having reflected on how I am known (or perceived) by others, I realized that I have never been alone in my life's journey! In my early childhood, I was nourished, clothed, sheltered and protected. As I grew older, I was educated and guided; nourishment and protection continued. As an adult, although I assumed the role of nourisher and protector, I have been the recipient of many more kinds of nourishment and protection from my family, friends and associates.

But, most importantly, I have been blessed with the "unconditional love" of God. I can tell you, my brothers and sisters, I have had my share of "darkest days," days when I felt totally abandoned, filled with fear and not knowing what to do.

My dear friends, in past letters and conversations, I have said, "You can't change the past, but you certainly can learn from it." Now as you continue 're-journeying' or tell your story, what part of your life would you like to change? Would this change help you to become the person you would like to be known?

I pray that God will help you on your journey as you search to discover the meaning and purpose of your life.

Chaplain

"No act of kindness, no matter how small, is ever wasted!"

Aesop

December 14, 2007

Dear Brothers and Sisters,

As we continue our preparations for the celebration of Christmas Day and the celebration of Jesus in our lives, I wish to share a conversation I had last month while visiting with one of the men at the Justice Center. During our discussion, he compared himself to what he was before he came to the Center and to how he saw himself now. Before he was controlled by drugs and alcohol and, in his words, he was "a mean-spirited beast!" He was totally about himself and he had no self-control.

Now that he has been taken off the street, by the grace of God, he sees himself in a very different light and is grateful for having been given the chance to see how truly messed up his life was and how it was hurting those who really care about him. As a chaplain listening to his story, I was overcome by this young man's humble admission of his past transgressions and his resolve to clean up his act. As he said, "It won't be easy, but it is the right thing to do." As strange as this may sound, this was and is a great moment for this young man to recognize his own worth. He has truly found favor with the Lord!

Boris Pasternak is quoted as saying,

> "When a great moment knocks at the door of your life, it is often no louder than the beating of your heart, and it is very easy to miss it."

I believe, the young man I visited "heard the knock at the door of his life." I pray that he will continue to listen, to pray, and to resolve to do what he must to allow his real person to come alive and to live for and with those close to his heart.

My brothers and sisters, this is what the time of Advent is all about: discovering where we were, where we ought to be and what we need to do to make the changes that will help us truly celebrate in the silence of our hearts the coming of the Lord Jesus.

I am mindful and encouraged by the story of the Good Shepherd who left the ninety-nine to go find the one sheep that was lost and when He found the sheep, there was great celebration!

Wishing for you the Peace, the Presence, and the Power of God in your life always.

Chaplain

Dear Brothers and Sisters,

Now is the time to open our eyes! Now is the time to prepare, to receive "The Light of the World!" In an effort to relate, to understand, to appreciate and to embrace fully Our Lord and Savior into our hearts, let us reflect upon darkness and light.

When I was a child, I was quite fearful of having to go out into darkness alone at night. For me, this was a fear-filled time. My mind would conjure all sorts of evil people lurking in the darkness to do me harm. Although a few streetlights offered some rays of light, they also were accompanied by fearful shadows. It was always a relief to arrive safely into the confines of the house.

But, then there were places of darkness I had to encounter inside the house. Sometimes I had to go to the basement cellar to get some canned food my mother needed from the darkened pantry area. Then there was the nightly trek to the attic where I slept. These inside the house dark places preyed upon my vivid imagination and fears.

As I grew older these fears diminished but these physical fears gave way to other kinds of fear. The fear of loss touched many areas of my personal, professional, family, social, spiritual, and recreational life and often resulted in periods of great anxiety, a sense of doom and gloom. However, I have learned that where there has been "darkness" in any part of my life, it has been and is offset by the enlightenment and support of caring and understanding people, of a God who loves us unconditionally!

John O'Donohue in *Anam Cara* (a book of Celtic wisdom) writes vividly about the contrast between light and darkness. While reflecting upon his presentation of the contrast between light and darkness, I thought about the ups and downs, the fears and the hopes of my spiritual life, my relationship with the Lord.

My brothers and sisters, let me suggest that you examine your past and present life to identify the fears past and the fears present in your life. This we will call the darkness.

Let us open our eyes to God who shines Light upon us and dispels all darkness!

Chaplain

NAMASTE! I greet the God within you.

February 1, 2008

Dear Brothers and Sisters,

Last Friday I was not able to visit with you due to an emergency. Now it appears that I will not be visiting this week. However, I do want to share with you some of the blessings I have received during this time. First let me explain that I have had a serious bout with kidney stones. I was hopeful that this would all be behind me by the first of February, but my body dictates otherwise. Hopefully with your prayers and lots of patience I will be back to visiting next week, February 8th.

I started this letter with the Indian greeting because I saw and experienced God in so many ways since January 25th. It all started with the concerned, caring and loving ways of my wife. She spent longs hours by my side and then when I came home she not only took care of me but took charge of running the house. I wasn't permitted to do anything but rest.

Since leaving the hospital on Saturday and again on Monday, I am truly humbled by the various doctors, nurses and staff members who assisted me in the recovery process. Truly, through them I was greeted by God. The members of my family and friends who reached out to me by phone, cards and visits touched me in a similar manner. I recalled in one of my recent letters I said, "We don't hear God because we are at times too full of ourselves. Now I have had plenty of time to listen and to hear God speak through so many different people."

I believe these past eight days have restored by ability to recognize the reality and blessings that come through others.

My brothers and sisters, be assured of my prayers and love for you. I am especially appreciative of the many ways you have graced my life. NAMASTE.

Chaplain

Dear Brothers and Sisters,

I'd like to begin today's letter with a few questions, questions, I hope you will think about and, perhaps, your answers will be for you moments of grace. Who are you? Who do people say you are? How did you come to know yourself? Truly, do you know who you are? How do you feel about you? How would you describe your relationship with God? Are you pleased with what others say or have said about you? If you could change any part of your life, what would it be? What motivates you or inspires you to take action?

These are but a few of the many questions we may ask or others may ask of us in getting to know ourselves or others better than we know now. You might be wondering what has prompted me to begin with all these questions.

Since my visit last week, I have been thinking a lot about what some of you shared with me regarding your personal lives and/or relationships that you have been experiencing with your court-appointed attorney. I realize that the behavior of other inmates or some officers have in some cases added to the stress or anxiety that you have or are experiencing. Then there are those who have been abandoned or cut off from members of their family or loved ones. These personal stories have touched me deeply. I have been praying for guidance in how to respond to such very real pain, depression, and anxiety. And, the truth must be told! I don't have a 'one size fits all' answer.

My friends, I believe that in those difficult moments of our life in which we experience some pain or suffering are the times our faith may be challenged. As a faith-filled people, these are the times to remind ourselves that "Once you were 'no people' but now you are God's people; you 'had not received mercy' but now you have received mercy." (1 Peter 2:10)

Brothers and Sisters, rejoice in the Good News, God has not overlooked nor ignored us!

Chaplain

"At the sight of the crowds, his heart was moved with pity for them because they were troubled and abandoned, like sheep without a shepherd."

Gospel of Matthew 9:36

June 20, 2008

Dear Brothers and Sisters,

As I was sitting in Church this past Sunday and while fulfilling my promise to pray for you, I was struck by the Apostle Matthew's words: "...they were troubled and abandoned." I thought about many of the stories that have been shared with me by you, men and women at the Justice Center. So often you have experienced this very same feeling that Matthew speaks about. The 'troubling' feeling begins at the very first moment of arrest and continues until your case is adjudicated. Then begins a whole new series of 'troubling' (worrisome) concerns. I believe these troublesome times in and of itself are bad enough; but, all too often, these painful realities are made worse by the experience of actual 'abandonment.'

I cannot begin to tell you how troubling and painful it has been and is for me to know that many of you have been abandoned by family members, friends, and other loved ones in your lives. Your expressed depression, worrisome words and tears of hurt are very much alive in my thoughts and prayers for you. In fact, the stories you have shared with me regarding the times you have felt troubled and abandoned were recalled to mind quite vividly in Sunday's reading taken from the book of the Prophet Jeremiah: "Yes, I hear the whisperings of many: 'Terror on every side! Denounce! let us denounce him!' All those who were my friends are on the watch for any misstep of mine. 'Perhaps he can be tricked; then we will prevail, and take our revenge on him.'" (Jeremiah 20:10)

The words "Terror on every side" is an experience that everyone has shared in one way or another. My dear friends what does one do or have you done when confronted with terror and abandonment in your lives? Although dealing with and not avoiding these emotional and spiritual trials hasn't always easy for you, with the help of prayer and wise counsel received through reading and the help of others ('bunkies,' psychologists, social workers, chaplain) you gained the strength needed to deal with these painful sufferings that have been a significant part of your confinement. I urge you, my friends, to continue to listen to the Good News of the Lord:

"But the LORD is with me, like a mighty champion: my persecutors will stumble, they will not prevail."

Jeremiah 20:11

Brothers and sisters, lift your hearts and minds, turn and face the Lord, and all your troubles and fears will be tendered by Love Himself.

Chaplain

August 10, 2008

Dear Brothers and Sisters,

In last week's letter, I raised the question:

"What would make you celebrate wildly without inhibitions?"

The unanimous response was "freedom."

There were various reflections shared by you during my visit at the Justice Center. The more I thought about your responses, I began to think of your replies in a more positive light. Instead of looking at and celebrating your release from incarceration, I thought each of you would be better served if you reviewed the changes that have taken place within your mind, heart, and resolve since the day the door of your freedom was shut, that is, your placement in the Justice Center. What are the significant changes that have occurred mentally, physically, emotionally, socially, and spiritually?

Pause, list, and reflect upon these changes. Are you pleased or concerned about the status of each?

It is true that one form of freedom has been taken from you, but I would like to point out to you that your have been gifted (graced) with another form of freedom! Although your 'normal' or usual way of living (lifestyle) has been temporarily taken from you, you been given time and opportunity to make some long overdue adjustment and changes in your life.

How, my brothers and sisters, are you using this time and opportunity for wholesome change?

This is not time to be used for making excuses for your shortcomings, nor blaming others for your poor choices or harboring hatred or resentment towards others.

Yes, it is true that at times you will experience loneliness or abandonment by God, family, and those significant others in your life. Nevertheless, you must not allow yourself to give up hope nor quit on your determination to become a better person.

Be ever assured of my concern and prayers for you.

Your Chaplain

Dear Brothers and Sisters,

There are two readings from the Bible, one from the Hebrew Scriptures (1 Kings 19:9, 11-13) and one from the New Testament (Matthew 14:22-33), that I would like for us to reflect upon. In the first reading, we heard the story of Elijah on the run from his persecutors. He has fled to the mountains and is hiding in a cave when God comes to him, and, we might say, comforts Elijah. In the second reading, while in their boat several miles off shore, the disciples are caught in a terrifying storm, and Jesus appears to them walking on the water. They become even more terrified thinking, as Jesus approaches them, that they are seeing a ghost. Jesus speaks to them,

"Take courage, it is I; do not be afraid."

Gospel of Matthew 14:27

Again, words of comfort are given. These stories bring to mind the many kinds of fear that may obsess us. What are those fears that may have caused us or may now cause us severe fright or flight or leave us with an overwhelming sense of hopelessness?

I can think of times when I worried about finding a job or keeping the job I had. Then were the times I feared for the health and needs of my wife and children. There were also financial and security issues that gave me many sleepless nights. And, as we grow older, fear of the unknown and the fear of death seem to be a constant companion.

Looking back to my past behavior, sometimes fear so obsessed me that "I wasn't me." I felt so alone, confused and, like Elijah, I was on the run! And, like Peter, I let those troubling fear-filled storms of my life so distract me that I did not trust God nor man. My spirits were truly permeated with doom and gloom. I want you to know that although others have often characterized me as being a very optimistic person, I have had many bouts with fear and my faith has often been shaken!

In sharing my thoughts on fear, I am reminded of a proverb attributed to the New Zealanders: "When you face the sun, the shadows will all be behind you." When I think of the sun, I think of the Lord, Jesus. The shadows are all those fears that cause us to turn away from Jesus, as did Peter; while walking on water, he allowed himself to be distracted by the strong stormy winds and he began to sink into the sea. Please note: Before Jesus rescued Peter, He chided him, "O you of little faith, why did you doubt?" (Gospel of Matthew 14:31b)

My brothers and sisters, I believe there is simple but profound lesson found in this story of Jesus, His disciples and especially Peter. Similarly, when God talks to Elijah, we note that God is not found in the wind, the fire, or the earthquakes but rather is heard in the quiet of our being. This is how the Lord is heard!

Let us face the Lord. Trust Him, believe in Him and all "your shadows" (FEARS) will be behind you.

Chaplain

"The unexamined life is not worth living."

Socrates

September 12, 2008

Dear Brothers and Sisters,

In past letters, I have challenged you and myself to describe ourselves. Who am I? What did I do? What am I about? What is the purpose in doing what I do now? Remembering what Jesus asked His disciples, "Who do the people say I am?" might be a good question to ask ourselves as we examine our lives. Having read books, listened to lectures, discussed and taken notes on the purpose and meaning of life, I have chosen the metaphor, travel, as a way to help me to share with you some discoveries I have made in attempting to understand the purpose and meaning of my life.

I would like to begin by examining the notion of travel. When I think about the word, travel, I think about the many different modes of travel, the duration of a planned trip, the purpose, the cost and the people who may go along on a trip. No matter the length of the trip to be taken, planning is important as well as knowing the destination and purpose of the journey to be undertaken. Whether I go on a trip alone or, accompanied, there is the issue of baggage. Today, more than ever, especially when traveling by air, excess baggage is costly. There has been a recent change in how many bags a person may check in at the airport as well as significant charges levied for extra baggage a person may wish to bring along for a trip. These days, the wise traveler travels lightly!

Travel lightly we must! Whether in our professional, personal or spiritual journey we must take time to examine closely the purpose of our trip in order to find the excess baggage we may be carrying. Like vacation travelers, we may be picking up more baggage (souvenirs, mementos) than we really need for our journey.

Looking back on my personal experiences, I find myself freed of a lot of baggage that used to weigh heavily upon me. In my professional work, fear of failure, anxiety about the expectations and perceptions that others may have had about me, being able to meet deadlines in a timely and acceptable manner were but a few of the many issues that I carried far too long. Striving, proving, providing, moving ahead are actions that affected me immensely as an every day worker. As a result, not only was my mental and emotional life stressed, but also my spiritual growth was affected. Now that I am retired, I am freed of much baggage I carried needlessly, baggage that at one time weighed heavily upon me.

My dear friends, I believe it is in our best interest to pay attention to Socrates words: "The unexamined life is not worth living."

From time to time it is a good idea to take time to identify what baggage is holding you back? What baggage is affecting your spiritual life? Are you overworked? Resentful? Bitter? Turn to the Lord and listen to the Psalmist:

"Oh, that today you would hear his voice
Do not harden your hearts"

Psalm 95:7d-8a

Turn your burden over to the Lord! He will hear you and He will alleviate that which needlessly burdens you and keeps you from truly enjoying your relationship with Him and your loved ones.

Chaplain

Come to the waters....

"With joy you will draw water
from the fountains of salvation"

Isaiah 12:3

January 16, 2009

Dear Brothers and Sisters,

Two weeks ago while visiting with one of the Muslim brothers, we talked about the gift of air, and how essential air is to our physical well-being. Without air we would surely die. The same can be said about water. As my brother said, "This is cause enough to be 'thankful.'"

Since meeting with him, I have thought a lot about air and our use and the manipulation of air to improve our living conditions. What can be said about air can also be said of water. When I looked up the definitions of both air and water, I was amazed to find so many meanings for these two words as they apply to our spiritual lives. I'd like to suggest that you take some time to reflect on these four words: Air, Water, Spirit, and Life.

Also, take some time to read Isaiah 55:1-11, which begins like this:

> "All you who are thirsty,
> come to the water!
> You who have no money,
> come, buy grain and eat;
> Come, buy grain without money [...]"

> Isaiah 55:1a-e

Brothers and sisters, with great gratitude, let us embrace these gifts, the water, the spirit, and the life that is offered and proclaimed by the prophet Isaiah.

Chaplain

April 17, 2009

Dear Brothers and Sisters,

"We don't have much time; you get in that line and I'll get in this one. Oh no, the cashier needs help. We should have stayed in the other line."

"The traffic is backed up. Let's take a short cut."

"Wait for me and don't be late."

"We should have left earlier; we'll be late."

Does any of this sound familiar? From our earliest age we begin showing or expressing our impatience with waiting:

"Are we there yet? How much longer do we have to go?"

"Hey, no cutting; wait your turn!"

Just wait! Be patient!

What's the big hurry? Why is it that we find ourselves so impatient when we find ourselves in lines with other people waiting to be served or assisted? While driving along expressways a person in the passing lane going under the speed limit oblivious to the cars following behind can be another cause for impatience let alone irritation. What makes my need so much greater than that of another person's need?

This past week I became intensely aware of how 'time-bound' I have become and the benefits that come with letting be. Before the visit of my son and his family, my wife and I took time to discuss and to commit to a plan to live in the present moment and to spend our time together worry-free of time; and, to be conscious of the needs of our son and his family.

The preparation my wife and I made proved to be a blessing for all of us. From the time the family arrived on Thursday evening until the following Tuesday morning we had the most relaxed and enjoyable time together. This was no easy feat! Getting five adults and three young children ready for meals, trips to Church, the park, the museum, and stadium and 'on time' is always a challenge; to do so without anxiety and impatience was the result of our commitment to be present to the needs of our guests and to enjoy their presence.

The calm and peace I experienced this past week with the family visit helped me to understand and to appreciate John's account of Jesus visit with the Apostles after He had risen from the dead. When Jesus appeared before the Apostle, He did not blame or criticize them for their conduct during his arrest, persecution and death; rather, He greeted them with the words,

> "Peace I leave with you; my peace I give to you. Not as the world gives do I give it to you. Do not let your hearts be troubled or afraid."

> Gospel of John 14:27

The lesson I learned is quite simple; just as Jesus was

non-judgmental and welcoming so too we are called (sent) to do the same for one another. Do what he did for us. Jesus taught us how to live, how to give, how to bring peace. Graciously, let others go before us. Let waiting become grace-filled moments, moments of peace and love.

Chaplain

May 1, 2009

Dear Brothers and Sisters,

Last week, while visiting the county jail, I met a new brother, a first-time offender, a veteran who had served two tours in Iraq. During our conversation, the phrase "collateral damage" and the word "divorce" called forth, unintentionally, a lot of painful memories from the relevant experiences of his life.

As he shared his story with me, I felt his pain and the pain of so many other men and women serving in the various branches of the military who have been indoctrinated and trained to take the life of another. I also learned and felt a deeper awareness of the depths of collateral damage as experienced by our veterans.

Our conversation made me keenly aware of how negligent our military leaders, government officials, and veterans administration have been in preparing these vets for re-entry into life on the home front.

During our conversation, my friend shared with me that he was divorced and in no way did he excuse himself or accuse his spouse. His error, if we could call it that, unfortunately, he was not prepared to deal with PTSD and its effect on his attitude and behavior towards others, and adjusting to the circumstances of his life. What he needed was a divorce or separation from the conduct that had become a wedge in all his relationships. I believe many of the problems of marriages, unemployment, homelessness, imprisonment, drugs and alcohol, could have, should have, been avoided by a comprehensive mental, physical, and psychological treatment given to our veterans before returning home.

As I reflected on the conversation with my young brother's sharing, I thought about the words of Jesus when He said,

> "No one can serve two masters. He will either hate one and love the other, or be devoted to one and despise the other."

Gospel of Matthew 6:24a-b

This causes me to ask, "Am I who I say I am or am I someone altogether different, a stranger even to myself?" Sometimes we do not want to be seen the way we really are. When I, or when we, look at the way we have or are living our lives, how have we acted towards our wrongdoings, our sins?

Brothers and sisters, let us be honest about who we are and divorce ourselves that which separates us from Our Lord, and others.

Let us be a hopeful people and let the prayer of the Psalmist be ours and, trustingly, ask the Lord to create a clean heart in me and a steadfast spirit renew within me!

Chaplain

"Once the game is over, the King and the Pawn go back in the same box."

Italian proverb

October 29, 2010

Dear Brothers and Sisters,

After my first visit with the men and women I meet at the Justice Center, I give them a "homework" assignment. That is, I ask them to tell me who they are in twenty-five words or less. If they need more words, that is okay. I also ask those whom I am visiting if they would take some time to assess or review all their relationships, God, family, friends, co-workers, neighbors, church community, etc.

The purpose of this exercise is to get each person to review and to reflect on what was, what is, and what will be. Through this process of reflection, hopefully, changes that need to be made will be identified. Dialogue and prayer are essential elements of this review process.

During my meeting, I am quick to note this is a normal and necessary process for everyone. No matter how old or young, no matter if we are working or retired, it is good for individuals to take some time out to review their relationships and the direction their lives may be going. Business organizations, health, education and religious groups often conduct periodic workshops, retreats, or conferences for their members in order to improve the operations or services of the organization or to prepare the membership for changes that are to be made.

Change happens and will continue to happen. Change is not easy; however, whether in our personal or professional lives change is very much a part of the process for growth. How we respond to change depends largely on how we perceive ourselves to be.

No matter what our way of living or the work we do, the way we perceive ourselves to be, whether rightly or wrongly so, will determine whether we will benefit or not by the changes that affect our relationships at home, the work place, or events in our lives involving others.

Brothers and sisters, my question to you is, "How do you perceive yourself to be?" In God's eyes we are all equal. All people are our peers! Do we really believe this and act like we believe we are equal? I believe, what frequently happens to many of us is we get caught up in the comparison game. We act in one of two ways.

One way is to be never satisfied with who we are or believe everyone else is so much better than us. In this way of thinking, we are merely pawns!

The other way of acting is to act without impunity. Such people have an inflated image of themselves and see themselves above the law and most certainly, better than anyone else. They are king and rule over everyone! "At the end of the game king and pawn are put back in the box!"

Let us pray for the gift of seeing ourselves as God sees us, as equals, as one body, as brothers and sisters.

Chaplain

December 29, 2010

Dear Brothers and Sisters,

As the year 2010 draws to its end, what may we conclude about how we have invested, lived, the gift of this passing year in our lives? How has it been? A good year? No different than the past years? On the other hand, perhaps your year has been a most remarkable year, a time well spent. Has it been a year of good decisions, a period of time marked with improved responsible choices made by you?

No matter how difficult or how successful the year 2010 has been for you, I would like to propose that you take some time before you get into next year, 2011, to set aside some quiet, reflective, time to do both a looking back and looking forward in assessing the state, the conditions, of your life...I ask you, "If you were in God's courtroom, how would you present your case?"

I believe, in giving your answers to this question and "How have you lived this past year?" you may discover what decisions of behavioral change you may need to make in regards to your relationships with God and others in your life.

The author Henry David Thoreau went into a self-imposed exile to live as a hermit at Walden Pond for two years. He went into the woods of Walden because he wished to live deliberately and purposefully. He sought to understand the essential facts of living and to discover what he could do about living his life in a meaningful way. Henry wrote in *Walden*,

> "I went to the woods because I wished to live deliberately, to front only the essential facts of life, and see if I could not learn what it had to teach, and not, when I came to die, discover that I had not lived."

Brothers and sisters, when we take time to reflect back about the life we are living, we do this to consider whether or not we are alive and life-giving in how we interact with others. God does care how we live and how we relate to one another.

No one else has your gifts, your set of talents, ideas and interests. You own all of them, and they can't be taken from you.

You may, however, get side-tracked by addiction, indecisiveness, immoral or selfish choices, and as a result you may end up agreeing and acting as the cynics of life saying, "Life isn't worth living," and doing nothing to change in your life what needs to be changed, wash your hands, throw in the towel and conclude, "Whatever!" This isn't why God gives us a second chance.

What will you do differently this year to live more deliberately and purposefully?

Chaplain

"To see myself all around, I need a three-way mirror: God, myself, and friends."

anonymous

February 1, 2012

Brothers and Sisters,

After visiting with you, I always carry with me, in my mind and heart what you have shared with me in our conversations or insights from the discussion we may have had during our time together. On occasion, when I come home my wife will inquire as to how my day went during my visit. At other times, I will share with her some letters I have received from my "band of brothers," a term of endearment I use for those with whom I correspond. Invariably, we will talk about the 'justice system' as it is or has been experienced through both my conversations with you at the Justice Center and by those with whom I correspond.

This past week, I felt a bit overwhelmed by the sharings, the openness, the trust with which, you, my brothers and sisters, shared your stories. The accounts of abandonment by family and friends, the uncertainty and stress caused by the confusing judicial process, and the anger felt by some and the humiliation caused by correction officers were painful to hear. Others expressed their loss of faith in God and shared a deep sense of hopelessness as they looked to their day in court and their future.

Why believe? Why hope? Why trust anyone? How can I, how do I respond to all these very real and painful personal experiences and feelings shared by you?

I would first like to talk about your relationship or understanding of God. When the circumstances of your life or the consequences of the choices you made are not what you expected, I believe it is extremely important not to blame God or others for the outcome even though it is hard to think otherwise. All too often we treat Our Father, God, as a lesser being, a shrunken God. This view of God is like looking at Him through the wrong end of a telescope; He appears unconcerned, detached, distant, and out of our reach. Actually, Our Lord, is just the opposite. He's concerned, ever present, and always within reach if we but choose to call upon Him.

At times, when you feel overwhelmed with depression, hopelessness, or abandonment by loved ones, when you feel like a total loser, you might consider what a coach once told me, "You are not finished when you lose (or feel like a loser), you are finished when you quit!" This was his way of telling me not to give up trying.

I do not want you to quit. You are a good person, graced in many ways by God. Each day pray to see yourself as God sees you, loving, lovable and with a purpose for being here. You are not a loser; give yourself a little more credit. Remember, God is with you always, and He reaches you through the people He sends your way. You do have reason to be hopeful and not to quit on God, your loved ones, or yourself.

Chaplain

"The Lord GOD opened my ear;
The Lord GOD is my help
therefore I am not disgraced;"

Isaiah 50:5a, 7a-b

September 1, 2012

Dear Brothers and Sisters,

Why do babies cry? Why are young people so hard to understand? Why is there so much discord in the world today? Why, at times, do we find it so difficult to give voice to our thoughts and feelings? Why are there so many voiceless people?

When people lose their ability to give voice to their personal needs and to be understood, they cry out to give vent to their frustration, their inability to communicate effectively. The Prophet Isaiah and Mark, the evangelist, offer us some insight as to how it is that one may go about finding one's voice. Isaiah says, "The Lord GOD opened my ear" ...that I may listen. (Isaiah 50:7a) Mark, in his account of Jesus healing the deaf man, writes, "He put his finger into the man's ears and, spitting, touched his tongue; then he looked up to heaven and groaned, and said to him, 'Ephphatha!' (that is, 'Be opened!') And [immediately] the man's ears were opened, his speech impediment was removed, and he spoke plainly." (Gospel of Mark 7:33b-35)

First comes the listening and then, eventually, the finding of one's voice!

It is always so fascinating to watch the growth of a baby's language: crying, babbling, finger pointing accompanied with grunts and single words, and eventually phrases and sentences. However, the child's voice remains very limited and it takes time for the child to truly find their voice. As children begin listening, they develop their ability to exercise and to find their voice.

By now, my brothers and sisters, you may be wondering, where am I going with all of this? If you are, I am glad you asked! During these past two weeks, while visiting at the jail, I experienced several situations at the jail when I lost my voice. How does one begin to console those who share their burden of loss, the death of a parent while incarcerated, the accidental shooting of a life-long friend, and the separation from a spouse and children?

I seem to go back and forth between feeling certain and uncertain about life. At times my life goes along smoothly and then the next moment everything seems so out of sync. So I find myself wondering, who am I to give advice or comfort to others?

Just maybe this is what Isaiah was experiencing and feeling when he prayed,

> "The Lord GOD is my help
> therefore I am not disgraced;"

> Isaiah 50:7a-b

Brothers and sisters, in those human, twisted, and confusing circumstances set upon us, let us take comfort in the Lord's promise, that He is with us always. (Matthew 28:20) Let us pray that He will open our hearts, minds, and ears so that we listen attentively and find our voice!

Chaplain

January 2, 2013

Dear Brothers and Sisters,

In my last letter and conversation with you, we discussed the need and the resolve to confront the giants in our lives that are holding us back from being true to ourselves. Some of the giants we recognized and talked about were fear, faith, forgiveness, and not feeling good about what we have done in our lives. These are and were no small topics of our discussions; in fact, many books have been written on all these topics. Fear and forgiveness, however, were the two topics most frequently discussed during my visits, and that is what I would like to write about in this letter.

From the very beginning, when we were arrested and confronted with the charges brought against us there were many, many overwhelming fear issues that we had to face. There was the fear of what was going to happen to us personally, to our family, our possessions, our work, our reputation, and the whole judicial process facing us. There were a whole variety of fearful mental, emotional, physical, and relational issues that were quite traumatizing.

My brothers and sisters, have you dealt with or how are you dealing with your fears? Have you identified your fears? Are you confronting them? How are you going about this confrontation? Have you come to terms with the official charges being held against you? It is my hope that you are being totally honest with yourself as you set about to properly represent (defend) yourself to your accuser, the prosecutor, and judge.

Fear is a normal response to any accusation made about you. But you must not let fear be so overwhelming that it clouds your thinking and decision-making. Face the truth fearlessly; acknowledge what you have done and have not done. All too often, I have been told there is this belief, "you are guilty until proven innocent." And, the imprisoned, so often, are made to feel they are not worthy of any mercy, understanding, or forgiveness. You must not accept this kind of characterization.

What you believe about yourself and what others believe about you are often two very different points of view. Truthfully, only you know the real you, and whether you are guilty or not of the charges against you. If there is some measure of guilt, I think it is extremely important for you to personally address the issue and begin by forgiving yourself and asking forgiveness of the ones offended. The purpose of self-forgiveness is to free one's self from fear and the self-destructive judgments that keep you captive in jails of your own making. Forgiveness, of self or others, is a tremendous challenge for most of us; however, when we do so, our burdens are lifted and in their place is personal freedom and peace of mind and body.

My dear friends, as you recognize and face your fears, may you have always the courage to face them honestly, fearlessly, prayerfully, and hopefully!

Chaplain

"Preach the Gospel always;
if necessary, use words."

St. Francis of Assisi

April 2, 2013

Dear Brothers and Sisters,

I want to thank each of you for helping me to live a purpose-filled life. Thank you for taking the time to read, to listen, and to share your concerns about your faith, your family, and the issues that concern you. I see myself as a fellow traveler and your sharing of your discoveries and the changes you desire to make as we travel are always so hopeful and encouraging. What St. Francis of Assisi said, "Preach the gospel always; if necessary, use words" makes a whole lot of sense. It is not so much what we say that is important, but rather what we do for one another. In fact, the good Lord told us to love one another.

My dear friends, wherever there is discord or separation among family and friends, humbly ask for pardon or be most generous in forgiving those most in need of your love. Let us all strive to me more God-like, life-giving, compassionate, and loving.

Chaplain

November 4, 2013

Dear Brothers and Sisters,

Yesterday, I had two religious, faith-filled celebrations, experiences that, as to their setting, are quite a contrast. At one, I attended mass at Bellarmine Chapel on the campus of Xavier University; the other celebration was at the Southern Ohio Correctional Facility, where I shared in the closing of the Seventeenth Kairos Retreat offered for the incarcerated men of that facility.

At mass, our celebrant asked the community three, thought-provoking, questions: Why are you here? What did you bring with you? What do you want to take away from here? These are very good questions one might ask oneself at any convening or special events one may be attending. During the closing of the Kairos retreat, the forty male participants were divided into five families or groups and each group had to answer three questions: Why did you sign up for Kairos? What did you expect to receive from the experience? What are you going to take way from this weekend?

The response of the men, all of whom did some profound soul-searching, whether in their group or through individual sharing evidenced the transforming power of "The Kairotic Moment," a God moment, for these men.

Many of these men gave witness to their past broken lives, lives that were dysfunctional and with little or no awareness of God or much family love. These men did not really have to say much to give witness to what they had gained and the transforming power they were experiencing. The openness, the trust, the faith, the love they shared was so, so, inspiring. I came away with the feeling they are now resolved to build God's house where all are welcome!

Chaplain

January 2, 2014

Dear Brothers and Sisters,

Lately, I have been thinking about a question: What makes a good parent, teacher, coach, advisor, or friend? What qualities do they have in common that makes them good, the very best? In either one of these roles, we guide, assist, or challenge those we care about by either word or action. Rudyard Kipling said, "Words are, of course, the most powerful drug used by mankind!" From experience, we know that drugs can either help or harm us depending upon how they are used or abused by the person offering or the person using them. I believe the same can be said about the words we use or the actions (body language included) we display in working or assisting those we have chosen or are responsible to help.

Thank you for hearing me. I love you!

Chaplain

Just imagine you are able
to make a difference in the world!

January 9, 2014

Dear Brothers and Sisters,

I have a 'tickler file' in which I keep a collection of what I consider significant prose and poetry and thought-provoking quotations, observations, comments gleaned from my research and readings over many years. I consider this to be my bank of wisdom, wisdom worthy of sharing with others. There are times when I experience emptiness, uncertainly, or not knowing exactly what it is I might share in a meaningful way with those for whom I write. These are the occasions I turn to my tickler file to look for inspiration of ideas worthy of exploring and sharing.

As we are at the start of a new year, 2014, it occurred to me that the new year is a time in which we make a personal assessment of how we have lived or are living our lives. Also, it is a time in which resolutions are made to address the needed changes that we have determined to make to improve our lives. Therefore, I would like for your consideration a more positive approach to considering who you are and how you approach the changes you are planning to make during the year, 2014. Please take some time to read this poem, "Imagine." After reading and reflecting on these words, how do you intend to make a difference in the world, your community, your family, and in your personal lifestyle?

Imagine

Be who you are
Practice what you know
Teach what you learn
And continue to grow
Just Imagine!
Just imagine that
You are smarter than you know
More courageous than you guess
Stronger than you feel
Healthier than you are aware of
More creative than you believe
More capable than you recognize
You are more powerful than you think
More attractive than you assume
Wiser than you suppose
More valuable than you have ever been told
And you are able to make a difference in the world
That you have not yet begun to realize
Just Imagine!

Author unknown

Brothers and Sisters, may this year be a most grace-filled time of delightful surprises for you and all of your loved ones, and may all of you make a significant difference this year of 2014.

Chaplain

"Set before you are fire and water;
to whatever you choose, stretch out your hand."

Sirach 15:16

February 2, 2014

Dear Brothers and Sisters,

Recently, I returned from a short trip to Florida. In one hour and thirty-seven minutes I experienced a radical climate change. I went from mounds of snow, frigid weather, and icy roads here in Cincinnati, Ohio, to the warm, welcoming summer-like weather of Orlando, Florida, replete with green lawns, flowers, and palm trees. I was struck by the contrast between the way the folks in the north and those in the south were living and how the weather affected the way we dressed ourselves and responded to the elements that surrounded us.

While in Sarasota, Florida, I saw and took pictures of the famous sculpture done by J. Seward Johnson, called, "Unconditional Surrender." This sculpture captured the famous celebratory kiss by a young sailor and nurse in New York's Times Square after Japan surrendered, which ended World War 2 on August 14, 1945.

The end of the war brought to an end over a dozen years of hardship experienced by our nation: the

Great Depression, hunger and unemployment, the War, the loss of many lives, and a radical change in the lives of the American people. The Atom Bomb, the Cold War, working women, family mobility, and many, many, changes in the way we saw ourselves as a people, as a nation, greatly altered our lives.

As I ponder all the changes that have taken place in the world and in my life since that declaration of peace in 1945, I cannot help but think about the many choices I have made over these many years and how those decisions brought me to this point in my life. I am very much at peace with my Lord, my family and friends. I did not gain this peace on my own. Early on the mentoring of my family, teachers, co-workers, friends, and so many others afforded me guidance, support, and became a major force in the influence and direction of my life.

William James reminded us that we can change our life by altering our attitude!

I owe a tremendous amount of gratitude for the formation of my attitude toward my faith and for the countless positive directions I have received my entire life.

Writer Joan Chittister helped me to recognize change as an invitation to see the many choices we have and to see the outcomes and consequences of the choices we have made and will be making. Sometimes the choice we will be called to make will be a life-altering decision. Whatever the outcome, whether it be an ordinary or extraordinary choice, know that you never have to be alone in your deciding!

"Set before you are fire and water;
to whatever you choose, stretch out your hand."

Sirach 15:16

Sirach reminds us that we are free to choose the direction we will go. The question is: Will we play with fire—or will we walk God's way?

Chaplain

"You are the light of the world. A city set on a mountain cannot be hidden."

Gospel of Matthew 5:14

February 16, 2014

Dear Brothers and Sisters,

I am really blessed by the friends I have. I would like to talk about some wisdom I gained from two of them these past couple of weeks.

The first is Tom. He is a spiritual director, a man educated and dedicated to the practice of helping others to deepen their relationship with the divine or to learn and to grow in their own spiritual journey. Tom is so much more than a friend. He is a go-to-person who truly, attentively listens as I, along with others, share our joys and setbacks in our life journeys. Tom by his intervention has helped me to understand and to appreciate the value of meditation and guidance.

My other friend is Pat. Pat and I have been friends for over sixty-five years. The two of us have been educators all our lifetime. Pat is special because of his honesty, integrity, wisdom and his willingness to always help those in need. In a recent response to one of my prison ministry letters, he made me aware of how so many people needlessly live lives in darkness and hurt and sadness.

As I reflected on the words and actions of my friends, I asked myself what may I and you do to help those brothers and sisters of ours who feel cut off from the rest of world because of the social, emotional, and spiritual poverty of their lives. What do we need in order to help those find their way out of their aloneness, their darkness?

While reading, studying, and searching for answers as to how we might respond, reach out to others, I found a good starting point in Matthew's Gospel when Jesus describes His disciples, those who would follow Him,

"You are the salt of the earth.
You are the light of the world."

Gospel of Matthew 5:13a, 14a

Therefore, we should live lives of openness and

involvement, a light and inspiration for all who are a part of our lives. Live by example. Walk the walk! Talk the walk!

Chaplain

May 1, 2014

Dear Brothers and Sisters,

When I was a kid, I wanted to be a Messenger Boy, one of those guys riding a bike who delivered important messages. Across the back of his shirt in bold letters was the word MESSENGER. These messengers' job was to deliver important documents that were urgent and needed immediate copy for signing or decision-making. In big cities like New York or Chicago there are still messengers to be seen delivering special messages that cannot be telephoned, faxed, or emailed. Messages delivered in this manner are more than time-saving, in many instances these messages carry life-saving needed information.

Today we are surrounded, through visual and print media, with many, many, messengers.

At the risk of sounding terribly naive, I believe God's voice comes to us through His word and through the words and actions of His people, His followers, those He sends to us, His messengers! In 1 Peter 2:20-25 is found an astounding account of how God, working through Peter, converted the hearts of three thousand listeners in one day! Peter, as we know, in fear three times denied his knowledge or relationship with Jesus. Peter later repented of his denial and dedicated, even to death, his life to telling his story and sharing Jesus' words to inspire others to not live mindlessly but to follow the voice of the Lord.

One fact is certain, the Lord knows and recognizes our voice.

> "In my distress I called out: LORD!
> I cried out to my God.
> From his temple he heard my voice;
> my cry to him reached his ears."

> Psalm 18:6 and also in 2 Samuel 22:7

Chaplain

November 5, 2014

Dear Brothers and Sisters,

Today I received a spiritual message from one of my nieces, who sends me one every day...today's thought: "You can't have perfect knowledge now but you can enjoy perfect love." How true, I thought!

I say this, because lately I have been thinking a whole lot about love. Actually, I have been enjoying love, God's love for me. Let me explain how this has been happening. As I drive down Galbraith Avenue on the way to the city, I see this enormous, beautiful fall-colored tree. Shimmering in the sun this amazing brilliant reddish-orange tree is alive with God's presence! I refer to this tree as 'my flaming bush.' Just as Moses had his flaming bush, I have mine! The beauty is this...God's beauty and presence is not limited to this one tree.

As I am riding along the road, I notice other colorful trees and as a result I feel like God is delightfully tree-hopping to be near me. It has become clear to me how near is our God to us and how dear we are to Him!

Love is a response to a call; it is yearning to be with another. Love, like Moses' flaming bush, burns without consuming. My brothers and sisters, which do you prefer, thinking about or experiencing the love of another, God's love for you?

Chaplain

February 3, 2015

Dear Brothers and Sisters,

A week ago today, while seated at the dinner table, my wife said to me, "I think I am going to faint!" I took her to a chair in the living room. While seated she began to experience intense chest pain and cried out, "It hurts, it hurts, call 911." Once Jean was placed in the ambulance it took about fifteen minutes before they drove to the hospital.

In the meanwhile, I was seated in my car waiting to follow. It was during this wait that I experienced a complete and uncontrollable melt-down. Clearly I realized the intimacy and strength of our love for each other. From Saturday evening until Wednesday afternoon the doctor tested, diagnosed, treated, and restored Jean's irregular heartbeat, Atrial Fibrillation, which had brought about this emergency.

We are truly grateful to all who were involved in helping in Jean's recovery. We are also appreciative of the outpouring of concern, visits, and prayers extended to us by family and friends.

During my visits, I will ask the brother or sister I am visiting, "How do you spell love?" As they spell the word, I write C-A-R-E. Then I counsel them to think about those people they care about and people who care about them...there is love!

Now, having experienced this life-changing experience and the outpouring of love, I realize I have not gone far enough in my thinking and understanding of the depths of love. The act of love, the gift of love, is so life-giving, unifying, healing, uplifting, and transformative...truly, words fall short in defining precisely what love is...but I do have a glimmer and an understanding of why Jesus said,

> "I give you a new commandment: love one another. As I have loved you, so you also should love one another."

Gospel of John 13:34

Love is manifest in actions. The writer of the Letter to the Hebrews was very much aware of the grace and power of love and that is why he urged the followers of Jesus,

> "We must consider how to rouse one another to love and good works."

Hebrews 10:24

My brothers and sisters, join me in singing: Praise the Lord who heals the broken hearted with His steadfast love!

Chaplain

Dear Brothers and Sisters,

Last week when speaking with many of you during my visit and after setting the stage to get your undivided attention, I asked you three questions: What is beauty? Are you beautiful? How would you describe your beauty?

Your responses to these questions, for the most part, were most positive and encouraging. Our discovery: we all are uniquely beautiful, and our beauty, when shared, compliments and shines forth in each other! This pleasant, life-giving moment is often experienced within our families, religious communities, and gatherings of friends.

What about those brothers and sisters who when asked these questions did not believe themselves to be beautiful nor did they feel loved by anyone. I was saddened by those who responded in an open, honest, and trusting way, shared their pain of loneliness and the uncertainties of their lives.

Since my visit, I have pondered...given much thought to these many personal responses to the questions of beauty...why do some feel so beautiful and others feel far from being beautiful? While thinking about how we perceive ourselves to be, I happened upon two sources of help this week that I want to share with all of my brothers and sisters.

The first is a question found on YouTube: What one word describes you? If you have access to a computer, answer the question...you will be prompted to other questions that affirm who you are! Very interesting!

The second source of help came from one of three small booklets excerpted from, *The Purpose Driven Life*, written by Rick Warren. His book is an invitation to question our existence, significance and purpose! In other words he asks us: Why am I alive? Does my life matter? What on earth am I here for?

When I think of all my connections through family, friends, work, education, church community, social, and you, I realize I have grown and continue grow because of all of you!

Chaplain

August 3, 2015

Dear Brothers and Sisters,

Today, our son and his loving wife and four children returned home after having visited with us for ten days. With them, my wife and I were able to share many wonderful experiences of our city, our church community, and many dear friends. The experience of this visit was a genuine revelation for me of how graced I am by my faith community, my family, and my friends...each group has been and is a special grace, a gift from Our Father, God.

Someone once asked: How can we know God better?

At the risk of sounding naive, I believe the answer is quite simple. We must become aware of the gifts that surround us or are being offered to us; this is a step in the direction of knowing God.

St. Teresa of Avila wrote,

"A good means of knowing God is to speak with God's friends."

In reading the Bible, we not only have an account of Jesus' words and works but also of his friends the Apostles and his many disciples who share their experiences and the lessons they learned from living with or following Jesus' teachings. Jesus revealed God through his words and works.

Accept and open the gifts that surround you everyday. Let the Father's gifts draw you ever closer to Him and really get to know Him!

Chaplain

October 1, 2015

Dear Brothers and Sisters,

Do you remember when you were in elementary school when a teacher asked you, "What do you want to be?" When I was a boy, most boys probably answered, "A fireman, a policeman, a soldier, a doctor, or a professional ball player." And the girls responded,

"A nurse, a teacher, a dancer, a singer, or a movie star." As for me, I wanted to be fighter pilot, a boxer, or a professional football player.

Looking back, I know my choices were very much influenced by the time in which I lived. I was seven when World War 2 began with the bombing of Pearl Harbor, and I was exposed to many war movies and all sorts of propaganda so I know these experiences greatly influenced my wanting to be a fighter pilot. Later, as a freshman in high school, a teacher told me that he thought I would make a good teacher, and he invited me to attend a preparatory high school to become a religious teacher.

Looking back over my life's work experiences, I can't help but ask, what was it my teacher saw in me that motivated him to invite me to consider becoming a teacher? I did become a teacher, and for over sixty years dedicated my talents to a life of service as a teacher in some capacity...as a teacher, coach, counselor, administrator, prison chaplain. In some ways I was like the blind man, Bartimaeus, who Mark writes about in his gospel (Mark 10:46-52). One day as Jesus was leaving Jericho, this blind beggar, hearing that Jesus was passing by, kept calling out to Jesus until Jesus stopped and asked Bartimaeus to come forth.

> "Jesus said to him in reply, 'What do you want me to do for you?' The blind man replied to him, 'Master, I want to see.'"

> Gospel of Mark 10:51

Miraculously his sight was restored.

When I look back to that time when I was invited to consider teaching as a career, I must tell you I would not have considered myself to be even remotely a possible candidate for teaching. No one in my family had finished high school, I was just an average student academically, small of stature and very shy and was not active in any school clubs or organizations. I certainly was blind to my potential as an educator. But, fortunately, I was graced by a dedicated and caring teacher to see what I could not see.

Brothers and sisters, what is it now that the Lord sees about you that you cannot see? What is your blind spot? Do you feel somewhat lost or uncertain about your present situation? May I suggest, like Bartimaeus, you call out to the Lord for His ear to hear your plea, and when asked the question, "'What do you want Me to do for you?" place yourself in His hands and plea, "Master, I want to see."

Chaplain

November 2, 2015

Dear Brothers and Sisters,

When corresponding with one of my brother friends, he would always end his letter with a wish for me - "May you always have enough." I would end my letters to him - "May you have enough plus."

To this day I cannot explain why I added the "plus."

Perhaps being aware of his separation from family and loved ones or perhaps of the many material setbacks he and his family were experiencing during his incarceration that prompted me to wish him all that he had before.

Later, I learned the wisdom of his grace-filled wish for me. Think about this for a moment. If I have more than I need, there is the temptation to want more...to become so greedy that I think myself so independent that I become blind to how indebted I am to Our Father, God. But, by wishing for enough, I am content and thankful for what I have and never lose sight of the fact that I am what I am and have what I have by the grace of God.

With the annual celebration of our National Holiday, Thanksgiving Day, just a few days away, I would like to share some reflections from past Thanksgiving Day letters I have written.

> What have I harvested this year? For what, for whom, am I grateful? Realizing how special and sacred each day is, the attitude of gratitude is the one to daily keep in mind.

> This Thanksgiving Day, be alive! Slow down! Consider this: for you, what is the real meaning of Thanksgiving? Is it really for whom Thanksgiving is all about?

> My friends, as you discover what God is up to in your lives and as you grow in your understanding of God's Word, may you stumble less and draw closer to Him.

"Give thanks to the LORD, for he is good,
his mercy endures forever."

Psalm 118:1

> As we prepare to celebrate Thanksgiving Day, let us remember in our minds, hearts, and prayers all our teachers, especially our parents, our first teachers, and give thanks to Jesus who taught us how to live and to care (love) for each other.

> When there is nothing left but God, this is when we find out that God is all we need!

Brothers and sisters, each day let us pray to be open to the spirit of God and to see the good around us, within us, and to be ever thankful. And, let us continue to make music in our hearts, always thanking God, Our Father, for all the many graces of love He bestows upon us.

Chaplain Jack

June 10, 2016

Dear Brothers and Sisters,

Recently my wife and I were reviewing pictures of our grandson from the time he was an infant up to a recent graduation picture. I found it quite fascinating to look at all these pictures of our grandson from the time he was an infant until now a high school freshman to be. The transformation that has taken place is truly fascinating and quite amazing.

This singular evolution of an infant becoming a very special teenager has evoked much thought and many questions about the transformations that are taking place in our lives daily. Ponder for a moment your own growth and development...your transformation... over the years. No matter who you are, please note, you did not become who you are now without the care and support or some challenges and resistance from many, many, people in your lifetime. This changing, transforming, is ongoing and hardly noticeable to others.

One of the most dramatic and radical changes we read about in the Bible is that of Saul who notoriously set about persecuting the followers of Jesus. In Galatians 1:1-19, Saul, who is re-named Paul, confesses how at one time he persecuted Christians and then he writes about his re-birth, his transformation in becoming a follower of Jesus. After his conversion of heart, Paul took up the cause of Christianity with the same devotedness and intensity as he had had while persecuting Christians.

Last week while visiting with one of my brothers, I suggested that instead of saying, "How is it going?" we might consider changing to "How are you transforming?" Or we might want to add excitement to our greeting and say something like: "Wow, what an awesome transformation, God has certainly paid you a visit!"

Chaplain

Dear Brothers and Sisters,

At the start of this letter about choice, the joy-filled, grace-filled events of the past five days dominate my thinking and my gratitude for a choice I made on December 30, 1970, when I married my wife, Jean, and officially became a member of the Henry and Elizabeth Hoelting family. Every four years the family gathers for a reunion held in Nazareth, Texas, a small German-Catholic farm community of three hundred and eleven. At the last reunion (2012) the family numbered 1010. At our recent gathering, we now number 1152+2 (two births took place during the reunion).

There were 537 present for this three-day celebration! Words cannot adequately describe this family of so many gifts and graces...hospitality, graciousness, caring, compassionate, inspiring, supporting, and a spiritually-joyful group of all ages reaching out and embracing all with much love and understanding. I am ever so grateful for the choice I made in 1970 having absolutely no idea of the life that I would and have enjoyed over these many years.

Perhaps now is a good time to assess where our priorities are? How do we personally interact with God? When we pray, do we lift our minds and heart to God? Have we chosen to bond with God in all that we do?

Chaplain

Dear Brothers and Sisters,

Reflecting on the readings from church last Sunday, I thought about my life, the lives of my family and friends, and the lives of so many people I have visited or corresponded with who are incarcerated. Without exception, we all have or have had our personal struggles, our crosses to bear. And, so many times our well thought out plans fail to accomplish our desired goals.

At first, the church readings seemed so depressing, so dreadful. But, as I reconsidered them, I realized that in dealing with all my struggles and in the darkest of times, I have never been alone. Somehow I always received help to work out the difficulties or challenges I have faced with divine intervention and the generosity of the Lord's faithful servants.

Speaking of 'divine intervention' I would like to share with you an experience I had on the golf course the other day. At the turn, a delightful young man asked to join our foursome but we offered to let him play through. The groups ahead of us were backed up causing the young man to play with us for about four holes before he could move on ahead. During his short stay with us, I discovered he had spent a short time in jail and that he was a recovering alcoholic. I was talking with him about ball markings; he shared with me his special marking ABR...Ask, Believe, and

Receive. This he said had changed his life..."I am now nine months sober and the happiest I have ever been." The brief encounter with the young man reminded me of The Serenity Prayer that is often prayed by recovering addicts. "God, grant me the serenity to accept the things I cannot change, courage to change the things I can, and wisdom to know the difference."

In our struggles with changes taking place in our lives, may we be graced with the serenity of acceptance, courage, and wisdom to learn and to follow always the Lord's Word, ABR.

Chaplain

God Cares About All His People —
read all of Psalm 139!

"Even before a word is on my tongue,
LORD, you know it all."

Psalm 139:4

July 7, 2017

Dear Brothers and Sisters,

In my last letter I wrote to you about becoming peacemakers, that is, living in peace now! After discussing this letter with many of you, I realized how aware I became of one of the biggest impediments to peace...passing judgments on others and how this can and does interfere with building any of our relationships and ultimately lessens peace in our homes, workplace, and communities.

Have you ever found yourself with a group of people and a new person (a first timer) enters the gathering event or room (or pod) and before you are introduced to this person, what happens with you or the other people in the group? At once, we begin to make judgments or evaluations of this new person. We start with the person's appearance and as this person speaks and interacts with others, further judgments are made as to what may be acceptable or unacceptable about the newcomer.

This I would say is a quite natural behavior. However, I feel, often times there is a real danger of making snap judgments of another that are for the most part an unfair discount that prevents one from truly knowing a person. On the other hand, if we put aside first impressions and make a sincere effort to greet this person with an open mind and a welcoming heart, I believe we will be for the most part pleasantly surprised about what we come to discover and know about those for whom we refrain from judging by appearances or our own biases.

Sisters and brothers, to help us guard against unfair judgment of others let each of us develop a mindset like our God who loves all.

Chaplain

"They that hope in the LORD will renew their strength,
they will soar on eagles' wings;
They will run and not grow weary,
walk and not grow faint."

Isaiah 40:31

September 20, 2017

Dear Brothers and Sisters,

Last Friday was a very special day. I met a young man at the county jail who admitted to me that he is an addict. He shared his story of addiction and the pain and suffering this brought upon him and his family. Furthermore, while in jail, he not only found and welcomed God back into his life, but also has made a plan to dedicate his life to helping others struggling with addiction by sharing his story.

In his sharing, this man said that he wanted so much to learn about how to pray. Prayer, I told him, is basically conversation with God. It is doing just what you and I are doing right now...sharing, questioning, seeking, being joyful, and sharing whatever issues we may have that are troubling us or causing concern or fear. The difference is our conversation is with Our Father, God, and not with each other. Experiencing the light in this young man's eyes and hearing his heart-felt words, I could not help but feel God's presence within him.

Later, on Friday evening, my wife and I joined members of our church community to participate in a Taize prayer service. The theme of the prayer service was healing. In light of the many recent events in our nation, we prayed especially for the gifts of peace, justice, healing, and we acknowledged the hurt and suffering of so many in our country caused by addiction, racism, hurricanes, earthquakes, floods, fire, and political divisions. The simplicity and deeply touching, heart-filled prayers of the Taize service was just the remedy for my spiritually-parched, aching soul.

Chaplain

January 23, 2018

Dear Brothers and Sisters,

One of my wife's favorite pastimes is putting together jigsaw puzzles, and I must admit, I am easily persuaded to help. We have successfully accepted many challenging puzzles...puzzles in the shape of a pizza or a bald eagle, a 1000-piece puzzle with every piece having a straight edge, a 3D stand-up puzzle and a few puzzles having two and three thousand pieces. I must tell you, the two of us always have immense satisfaction upon putting the picture together. After finishing the puzzle, we sometimes mount and frame them but most often we disconnect all the pieces and put them back in a box...the experience becomes a memory. Why am I telling you this about one of my wife's favorite pastimes?   Because last week I came across a reflection written by Darci Sims found in the January 15, 2018 edition of *Sound Bites Ministry*. Her story is a metaphor of life as we know and experience it, and one that I wanted to share with you.

Darci questions why her life feels like a 1000-piece puzzle with so many experiences of loss and difficulty while everyone else's life seems so put together. She notes the pain of these pieces feeling so scattered but then the wisdom of picking up each piece and wondering how all these pieces might fit together again — maybe to create a whole new picture.

Friends, we do have a choice...open up and begin to put together the pieces of your puzzle with help from God, family, friends, and others who love you.

Chaplain

Dear Brothers and Sisters,

During my weekly visits to the jail, I meet with a small group of men at their quiet time for reflection, discussion and prayer. Last week before the close of our gathering, one of the men asked, "What is it like to live with someone you love and to be loved by them?"

I do not recall my response to this young man's profound question, but since then, I have given his question much thought and reflection. I do remember telling him a good love relationship is so life-giving, but it requires attentiveness and maintenance. Often times, like any relationship, the love we have for and with another can be lost by neglect. Therefore, if we truly appreciate and value the love we have for our spouse, fiancé or fiancée, friend, fellow-worker, or God, then we must listen to the verbal and non-verbal signals sent our way from those who love us and whom we love in return.

In order for us to truly enjoy an inter-active, life-giving, relationship, it is important to know, to love, and to embrace the unique and special person I am. We are here on earth to be the special gifts God created. No two of us are created the same; each of us is special. Therefore, it is very important that we no longer live a divided life, that is, I no longer live on the outside in a way that contradicts what I believe in my heart. I will no longer act as if I am a half-person. I will be true to myself.

Chaplain

"Ask and it will be given to you; seek and you will find; knock and the door will be opened to you."

Gospel of Matthew 7:7

December 10, 2018

Dear Brothers and Sisters,

One of you shared with me, "Jack, you said, '...believe me, God does hear and answers all our prayers... having said this, I want you know this takes patience, trust, and listening and recognizing the messages and messengers that He sends to answer your requests!' I keep listening...give me a sign...but I'm not sure things are changing. I mean, I'm ten years into my sentence and I suppose I could keep listening for another twenty years and eventually things will have to change, but that's not acceptable to me. However, every day thousands of people die, more are born; people get shot, get sick, or overdose. What about their needs? Sometimes I think I'm not exactly on God's priority list since people with more important issues (death!) get ignored just the same. See, I want to believe...I guess you're just a better man than I am in that aspect."

Wow...brother, where do I begin to address your feelings about faith as you are experiencing it now? Let me begin by saying, 'comparisons are odious!'

No, my friend, I am not a better man than you when

it come to our Father God. I, too, ask myself, "Why, Lord?" when I see such senseless loss of life done by terrorists, dictators, gangs, and other violent acts perpetrated upon the innocent. Then we have all these natural disasters like earthquakes, floods, mudslides, fires, tornados, tsunamis causing great loses and taking many lives, and I find myself once again asking, "Why them and not me?" I see so, so, many homeless people on our street corners standing and begging for help... and there is all this talk about unemployment at an all--time low and wages at an all-time high and I wonder why and who is or isn't telling the truth?

My friend, I hope you see that I am so much like you... there is so much about our lives...the inequities, the injustices, the haves and the have-nots, the rich and the marginalized, the length of your sentence...it can be so overwhelming...but WE CAN'T GIVE UP ON THE LORD!

It may help to say the Serenity Prayer each day:

> "God, help me to accept the things I cannot change, the courage to change the things I can, and the wisdom to know the difference."

Our faith enables us to transcend that which we cannot understand, reason, or begin to fathom...faith without good works is dead...we are called to help out our brothers and sisters in need...not judge them...let Our Father use us as His messengers to bring hope and answer to others' prayers of need. Jesus told us,

> "Look at the birds in the sky; they do not sow or reap, they gather nothing into barns, yet your

heavenly Father feeds them. Are not you more important than they? Can any of you by worrying add a single moment to your life-span?"

Gospel of Matthew 6:26-27

Our Father will not forsake you.

Trust me, my friend -

"Ask and it will be given to you."

Gospel of Matthew 7:7

Chaplain

August 9, 2019

Dear Brothers and Sisters,

This past weekend I had an unforeseen, certainly not planned, stay in the hospital. Actually, apart from the medical reason, the stay proved to be for me a spiritual retreat...a blessing in disguise. In this letter I want to share with you some words I either read or heard and some thoughts about God's love for us and the imperative for us to share the Father's unique love for each of us with each other.

Late Saturday afternoon my wife drove me to the emergency room at a local hospital. Later, we were informed that I would be kept overnight. After my wife left to return home that evening, I turned on the TV only to be shocked by the news of the most senseless horrific loss of life in the City of El Paso, Texas. It wasn't much later that a special report announced the 1 a.m. shooting in Dayton, Ohio, in which nine people were killed in thirty seconds before the shooter was shot dead. The suffering of so many victims along with that of their family and friends was too much for me to absorb let alone to comprehend. I shut off the TV and prayed.

While praying, I put myself in the Holy Presence of God and I asked Jesus if He would sit between my wife and me and silently hold our hands. He did! Not only did I experience the depths of God's love for me but the love of my wife whom I have known for over fifty years. This singular experience was more than an epiphany; it was a transforming grace that I want to continue to share with my family, friends, and those I encounter in my ministry, my daily life.

Coincidentally, on Monday morning I heard a woman, a recovering cancer patient and a guest speaker on the *Today Show*, share a similar story. God's loving presence is what sustained her during the difficult and challenging journey to her full recovery. The times at night when she is in bed, and can't sleep, or at alone times during the day, she will stop and in the Presence of God and praise Him for the many gifts of life she receives daily. She deeply believes the love given her is meant to be shared with her family and others whom she meets each day.

On the nurse's computer monitor that was in my

room, all the rooms, the Mercy Hospital mission unfolds word by word as follows:

human dignity...
integrity...
compassion...
stewardship...
service.

Brothers and Sisters, I believe this message was no accident; this hospital mission for the staff spelled out for me how we can actualize the Father's message to love one another in and with His presence. Let us all practice the artful prayer of Presence!

Chaplain

Forgive one another...this is love in action!

September 5, 2020

Dear Brothers and Sisters,

Have you ever been in debt or made a loan and circumstances made it quite challenging to pay in full? Were you ever desperately in need of something and you went begging for help and you were met with thoughtful kindness? I have.

The first incident occurred when I borrowed a

thousand dollars on trust...no collateral. After three months, I was able to pay back three hundred dollars with the intent of paying the complete debt before the end of a year. About two weeks after I sent the money, I received a letter of forgiveness! When I opened the letter and read it, I had to sit down, I was so shaken with this surprise. I cried a lot by the thoughtful forgiveness of my indebtedness.

My other story of being a recipient of another's generosity happened on my trip in a borrowed car I drove from Milwaukee, Oregon to Murray, Kentucky. While I was driving very early one day, traveling through Cheyenne, Wyoming, suddenly the heat light on the dash lit up. I pulled over and discovered I was completely out of oil. Where I stopped along the highway, it was a very dry and desolate place. I happened to look across the road and there I saw an old trailer. When I went there and knocked on the door, no one answered. I just happened to look down and there left of a small step was a partly filled can of motor oil. I took it and used what amounted to be about a half quart of oil. This enabled me to get to the next rest stop. I asked a trucker if he might have some motor oil that I could buy. "No," he said, "you might ask the man in the camper over there." I did just that and when I asked the man for a can of oil, he gave me two cans. I offered to pay him for his kindness and he said, "No, just pay it forward; maybe some day you will be some one else's angel." I thanked him for his kind generosity and promised to do so.

I share these stories with you because of the theme 'forgiveness' as found in Matthew's gospel:

"Then Peter approaching asked him, 'Lord, if my brother sins against me, how often must I forgive him? As many as seven times?' Jesus answered, 'I say to you, not seven times but seventy-seven times.'"

Gospel of Matthew 18:21-22

Then just after this in the gospel, Jesus offers the parable of the servant who owed the King a great amount and fell to his knees and in great anguish asked for patience and he promised to pay all he owed the King. The King was touched by the servant's plea and forgave him the complete debt...but this servant turns around and refuses to forgive a fellow servant who owed a very small amount and the wicked servant had his fellow servant thrown into jail until he repaid all. The King wasn't a happy camper when he heard what this man had done!

Imagine your worse sin...in fact, all the sins you have confessed, and recall the relief, the joy, the gratitude you experienced when you received complete absolution for all your sins.

"Forgive your neighbor the wrong done to you; then when you pray, your own sins will be forgiven."

Sirach 28:2

"I give you a new commandment: love one another. As I have loved you, so you also should love one another."

Gospel of John 13:34

Chaplain

Dear Brothers and Sisters,

As an assistant principal in a large public high school, I was dean of discipline for ninth and tenth graders. Invariably one of the students would ask me, "Mr. K, why do you have that sign hanging in the window?" The sign held a simple truth, **God does not make junk**. This was always a great conversation starter.

"Tell me, what do you think it means?"

"Do you know your true value in God's eyes, you are priceless!"

"Don't sell yourself short...please! Invest your time well! With God you can do all things."

And, my favorite was a popular Elvis Presley song, "Put Your Hand in the Hand." If you do not know the song or have forgotten the melody, let me suggest you search the internet for the lyrics.

God does not make junk; in God's eyes all God's people are priceless.

Chaplain

A few words from Brian Shircliff, friend and curator of Jack's letters

We don't really know someone until they tell their story, now do we?

How I've come to know Jack Kennevan over the years has been interesting to say the least.

I knew Jack a bit from the church I used to attend, and then through friends, their annual parties. And when we doubled the size of the high school golf team I was coaching, I guess word got around that we needed more coaches. Jack called me and said he'd like to help. And that he did...his guys loved him as their coach.

I knew Jack had had a long and well-loved career as a teacher and counselor and coach and principal. I remembered him telling me once that long ago he was a Christian Brother and taught and was principal with that order for decades before marrying Jean and welcoming their ever-growing family...Shannon, Sean & Tina, four grandchildren.

Over the years after a couple of seasons coaching together, I'd see Jack at church or more friends' parties, long after our coaching days. He shared with me one of his letters to prisoners. I had no idea he'd been visiting incarcerated neighbors at our local jail. The letter was inspiring for sure.

And as inspired things do, new experiences drifted in the breeze to me that helped me understand better what Jack was doing and the tremendous need for more of what he and others were doing...

...one of our VITALITY yoga teachers began sharing yoga at a facility housing women mandated by the court to seek help with their addictions; it was such an awakening for me to visit this class so lovingly shared by this yoga teacher...

...and then an article found its way into my hands about how our prisons in the United States differ so much from prisons in Germany where prisoners live in open cells by day and cook their own meals together and are expected to use their time in prison to find ways that would never land them back there...perhaps a new career, new ways of dealing with life's stresses, new ways of being in relationship with family and neighbors...

...and then two friends found themselves in jail/prison. I tried to visit one of them at the very place Jack was offering his ministry all those years. I stood in line for hours on a holiday weekend, the only day my friend's own family was not able to visit, so they offered me their visiting slot while they used the time to settle a few things for him as he awaited trial. On that day I visited, I would guess there were about forty people ahead of me in line, eventually about the same number behind me...little kids hoping to see a parent, parents hoping to visit their son or daughter, friends hoping to offer their support.

If you walk by the street that faces the two towers of our county jail, you'll often see chalked messages on the sidewalks from friends and family. Sometimes there will be a gathering of people there screaming their love into the air and hoping their loved one will hear from inside their jail cell and look down at them on the sidewalk through the tiny slit of a window facing the street.

I looked at the faces of those gathered in this line to see their loved one, the time we all had to think as we waited. The line moved quite slowly, and then came a voice from around the corner where we actually checked in: "Twenty more minutes until we'll need to close for the weekend!"

I counted how many people were in front of me. The line moved very slowly. I turned around and looked at the faces of the children who would probably not be able to see their parent that day. Maybe for a longer time.

"Ten more minutes of check-in before we'll need to close this station. Once you're inside, you'll have about fifteen minutes."

I wondered if I should give up my spot for the family behind me. I wanted to see my friend, for sure, and he knew I was coming. I definitely didn't want to let him down. But these kids....

"Five more minutes."

The line moved forward. I rounded the corner and could now see where the voice was coming from, the check-in area where we were to sign in, offer identification, walk through the metal detector.

One more person and then it was my turn. I turned around and looked at the faces of the kids behind me.

"Alright, folks. I'm sorry, but that's all we can handle today."

There were gasps from many people behind me. Cries. Anger. Pain.

It struck me so quickly how ridiculous our system is in the United States. Not only does it punish the accused-offender — even more the accused who cannot post bail while awaiting trial — but especially the families and friends of those incarcerated in jails or in prisons all over the country.

And once inside and living the harsh and purposefully punishing life of jail or prison — and sometimes even harsher, solitary confinement — how little time or resource is geared to helping an inmate grow beyond this tragic chapter in their life. Even more tragic is the reality that prisoners once released and having served "their time" so often return to prison...their whole sentence never having helped them figure out a new path forward outside of prison. Many cannot find jobs with "felony" on their record. Many face the stigma of having been to prison...and then the silence of people who fear them or are anxious around them. Many find more belonging inside the prison than on the streets.

Truly, our system is broken.

And yet this jail I visited is where Jack was going every week for years. For more than a decade. I envision Jack sitting there at a table with an open chair, there offering light and love every week.

I see inmate after inmate sitting there with him. The conversations. The story each person shared. The love that Jack offered, no matter what. Jack called everyone 'brother' and 'sister' — family.

What a great gift Jack offered through his time and presence, and even more through the letter he painstakingly composed each week. Trying to get each word just right, trying to offer some gentle thing that might help each reader know they are loved, respected, called family...that's Jack.

As the systems we've inherited from past generations collapse or falter, perhaps we'll be brave enough to confront what we've inherited and enriched through our tax dollars with our current "rehabilitation and corrections system." Jack is quick to remind me that our nation stresses the "corrections" and too often forgets the "rehabilitation."

Other nations around the world have been so bold to create much different systems, perhaps with Germany leading a way forward that works short-term and, even more importantly, long-term.

Imagine that — Germany! The nation who only a century ago tragically and unjustly killed millions upon millions of people they had imprisoned.

And now Germany leads the world forward with new

possibilities where prisoners cook their meals together, share conversation and life and hopes and dreams, where "corrections officers" are trained for two years how to help prisoners figure out next steps essentially as counselors and career-coaches and encouragers, where each prisoner has their own cell with their own bathroom and telephone with which to call home, where prisoners go home for a meal a few times a year and then later an overnight and then later a whole weekend to begin growing into their new identity and career and life discovered while imprisoned. And this kind of "serving time" is no holiday — this is the hard and ever-important work of personal growth, of relationship.

Imagine.

We can too in the United States. If we are so bold. If we know the love from which Jack lives, from which he wrote all 290 letters...a love that motivated him to return week after week, year after year, no matter how soul-wrenching or inspiring, no matter not knowing who he'd meet each week, these brothers and sisters who would ask for him.

I hope you'll take a moment to search online for this very short article mentioned below and read it and be so moved by the delegation from our own country — some of the most conservative and some of the most liberal, some whose profession was caring for the incarcerated and some who were once incarcerated — who visited Germany together to learn.

It could be any of us who finds oneself in jail/prison, any of us at any time. An accident. A complete misunderstanding. You. Me. A family member. A neighbor. A dear friend. A total tragedy.

Wouldn't we want a system designed to help us find our way instead of one designed to punish us?

Wouldn't we want someone besides our lawyer and the court to hear our story, to witness our sharing of our story, someone who knows how to love us in such dire and tragic circumstances?

What if it were your loved one incarcerated, no matter if they were justly or unjustly accused?

Maybe all we need for a challenged system to change is a few more people to raise our voices, to call for a love like Jack offers his brothers and sisters, all of us.

Please check this out as soon as possible and join circles of neighbors desiring conversation and change:

What We Learned From German Prisons
by Nicholas Turner and Jeremy Travis
New York Times Aug 6, 2015
nytimes.com

VITALITY Cincinnati, Inc.

VITALITY is a circle of friends welcoming all, awakening each other, and reminding each other that we are Whole. Our affordable self-care programs invite everyone to move, to breathe, to rest, to contemplate, to grow...wherever each person begins their self-care journey, wherever and however they want to become.

donation-based drop-in classes...
in person & via Zoom

affordable trainings + individual sessions + volunteer opportunities

vitalitycincinnati.org

www.ingramcontent.com/pod-product-compliance
Lightning Source LLC
Chambersburg PA
CBHW071019120626
46546CB00003B/1156